all about cuts
and other hurts

Medical Consultant: Joel Buxbaum, M.D.

RITA GOLDEN GELMAN &
SUSAN KOVACS BUXBAUM

ouch!

all about
cuts
and other
hurts

Illustrations by Jan Pyk

Harcourt Brace Jovanovich

New York and London

Printed in the United States of America

First edition

B C D E F G H I J K

Library of Congress Cataloging in Publication Data

Gelman, Rita Golden.
Ouch! All about cuts and other hurts.

SUMMARY: Discusses what happens when the human body
sustains various minor injuries and describes its re-
actions to them.
1. Wounds—Juvenile literature. 2. Pain—Juvenile
literature. [1. Wounds. 2. Pain] I. Buxbaum, Susan
Kovacs, joint author. II. Pyk, Jan. 1934–
III. Title.
RD93.G44 617'.1 76-46310
ISBN 0-15-258839-6

For Lauren,
Steven,
Mitchell,
and Jan

contents

what is a hurt? 8

bee sting 10

black-and-blue mark 13

bump 18

burn 23

cut 30

eye, something in it 39

goosebumps 42

mosquito bite 47

nosebleed 50

pins and needles 52

splinter 56

stitches and scars 59

don't stop here 62

frequently used words and their
meanings 63

what is a hurt?

Cuts hurt. So do burns. A hurt is important. It lets your body know that something is wrong.

Whenever you feel a hurt, nerve endings are getting pinched or banged or burned or poked. Nerve endings are tiny,

8

stringy things that send messages to your brain.

Nerve endings are all over you. Many of them are just under your skin.

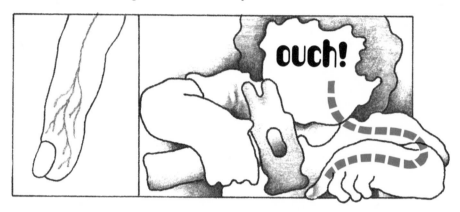

If you injure yourself, nerve endings send a message to your brain: "Ouch!" says the message. "Something bad is happening. Do something."

Once you know that something is happening, you can stop the injury from getting worse. You can pull your hand away from the fire. You can stop the knife from cutting you more. You can take care of a bleeding cut or remove a splinter.

Hurts can make you feel awful. But it's a good thing you have them.

bee sting

When a bee stings, it jabs its stinger into you and squeezes out a little bit of mild poison. As soon as the bee's poison touches your nerve endings, they send a message to your brain. "Ouch!"

The area around the sting gets red because extra blood rushes to the injury. The extra blood brings thousands of extra white blood cells. White blood cells are parts of your blood. Along with red blood cells, they travel in tiny hoses called blood vessels.

When the white blood cells get to the sting, many of them squirm out of the blood vessels in plasma. Plasma is the clear yellow, watery part of your blood.

White blood cells are your body's army. They fight anything that doesn't belong in your body. A bee's poison certainly doesn't belong in your body.

Thousands of white blood cells destroy the poison by gobbling it up.

All those white blood cells and plasma crowd together and make a lump where the sting is.

When the poison is gone, the white-blood-cell army and the lump go away. It usually takes a day or two before a bee sting disappears.

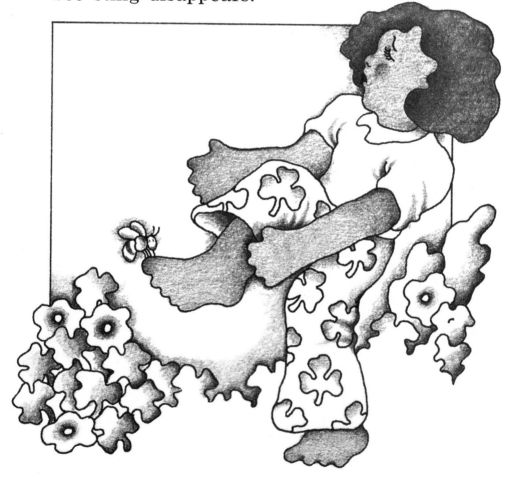

black-and-blue mark

Sometimes you bang yourself against something very hard, but you don't cut your skin. If the bang is hard enough, you may get a black-and-blue mark.

A black-and-blue mark happens when you injure a blood vessel under your skin and blood leaks out. A hard bang can cause a blood vessel to leak. The injured blood vessel patches itself up, but the blood that leaked out has no place to go. It is this spilled blood that causes a black-and-blue mark.

Blood belongs in a blood vessel. When it leaks out of a blood vessel, it is in a strange place. Whenever blood is in a strange place, it begins to change.

13

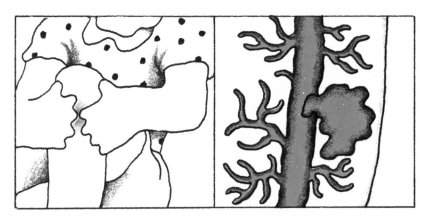

When you first bump yourself, the spot you bumped looks reddish. You are looking at the spilled blood through your skin.

Soon, the blood changes to a purple-blue color; your skin looks "black and blue." Your black-and-blue mark may turn green or yellow or brown before it goes away.

If your skin is light, you will be able to see the color changes clearly. If your skin is dark, you may not be able to see the colors as easily, but the same changes are taking place.

The spilled blood has to be cleaned up. White blood cells come to do the job.

Sometimes, white blood cells act like garbagemen. They wander around your body looking for garbage. When they find it, they swallow it up.

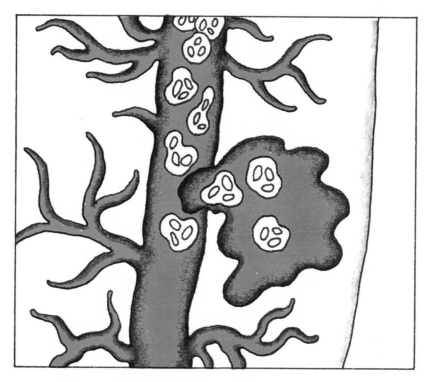

The changed blood is like garbage, and the white blood cells gobble it up. When all the blood has been eaten, the black-and-blue mark will be gone.

A *black eye* is a black-and-blue mark around your eye.

The curious thing about a black eye is that lots of times the broken blood vessel is not in the spot where your black eye is.

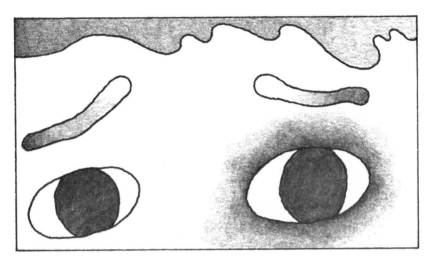

Suppose you bang your nose and injure
a blood vessel. The next day, you may
discover that you have a black eye ...
not a black nose.

Your eye gets black because there is a
lot of space around your eye. The spilled
blood goes there. It's sort of like a hole
in the ground when you dump a pail of
water nearby. The water finds its way to
the hole. That's what happens in a black
eye. The spilled blood oozes its way to
the space around your eye.

The black eye lasts until the spilled
blood is all cleaned up.

17

bump

A bang on your head almost always makes a bump.

Whenever you get banged, your body rushes white blood cells to the trouble spot. When the white blood cells get there, a lot of them squeeze out of the blood vessels in the watery plasma.

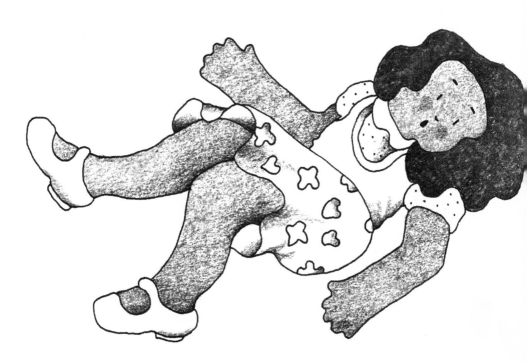

If you get a bang on your *arm*, the white blood cells and the plasma have plenty of mushy space to move around in. You hardly notice them.

But if the bang is on your *head*, the cells and the plasma don't have any space at all. Wherever they go, they bump into bone. The only place all those cells and all that plasma can go is out. And that's what they do ... causing a bump.

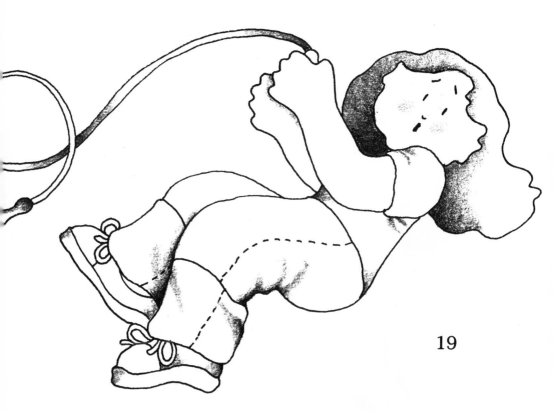

While they're there, the white blood cells have a job to do. The bang has injured tiny parts of you. The injured parts are no good anymore. They have to be cleaned up so new parts can take their place. The white blood cells do the clean-up job.

When the job is finished, the white blood cells and the plasma go back into the blood vessels, and the bump goes away.

burn

Burns hurt! If you are getting a burn on your hand, your nerve endings send a message to your brain. "Ouch! Something bad is happening. Do something!"

The first thing you do is yank your hand away. If your nerve endings didn't make you feel the hurt, you wouldn't pull your hand away. You would get a worse burn.

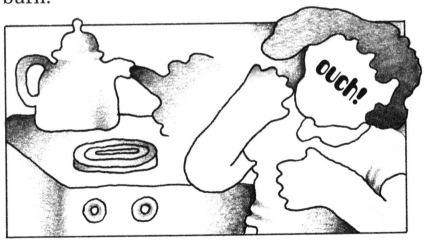

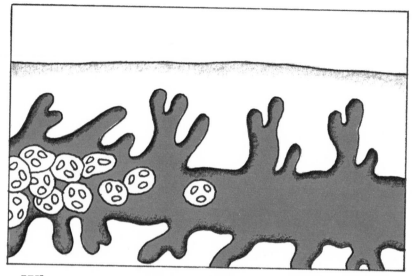

When you get a burn, blood vessels expand. Expanded blood vessels carry extra blood to your burn and make it look reddish.

You need more blood because a lot of tiny parts of you have been burned. The burned parts have to be cleaned up so new parts can be made. The cleanup is a job for white blood cells. Expanded blood vessels can rush thousands of extra white blood cells to your injury.

When white blood cells get to your burn, many of them squirm out of the

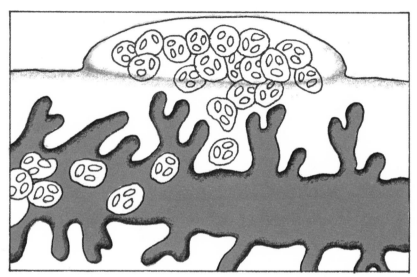

blood vessels, surrounded by plasma. They gather just under your burned skin. They make a soft, mushy pillow. That pillow of white blood cells and plasma is called a blister.

While the white blood cells clean up, your body works to replace the burned parts of you. When you are all repaired, the white blood cells and plasma squeeze back into the blood vessels, the blister disappears, and the burned skin falls off.

Burns can be very serious. A bad burn needs a doctor.

A *sunburn* is a burn, too. Some people hardly ever get a sunburn. Something called melanin protects them.

Everybody has melanin. It's a part of the skin. A person with dark skin has a lot of melanin. He or she can stay in the sun a long time before burning. A person

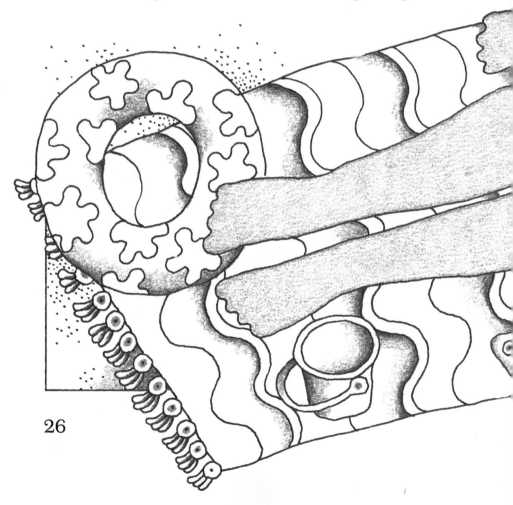

with very light skin has only a little melanin and can burn in just a few minutes.

Too much sun makes your blood vessels expand. When blood vessels expand, your skin looks reddish.

Like a regular burn, a bad sunburn will cause your army of white blood cells to squirm out of your blood vessels. Lots of blisters may pop up all over your burned skin.

A sunburn may peel. That's just the burned skin coming off after the burn is healed and the blisters have gone away.

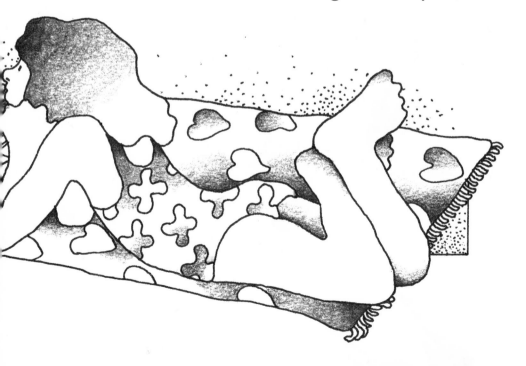

cut

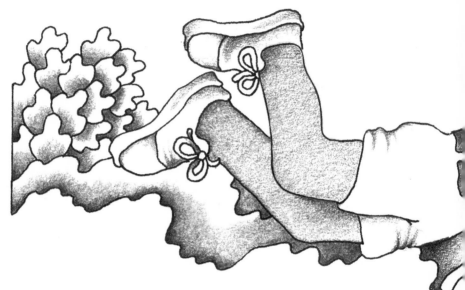

Cuts—everyone gets them. Most of the time, they're nothing at all. That's because your body knows how to take care of problems like cuts. And it does a terrific job.

If you scratch yourself, your scratch turns white. The white is dead epidermis that you have scraped up.

Your epidermis is the outside of your skin. It is made up of millions of tiny things called epidermis cells.

Epidermis cells sit around in piles. At the bottom of the pile are some especially smart epidermis cells, doing something very important. They are making more of themselves—all the time. Right this minute, they're snuggled up down there where you can't see them. They are busily making new epidermis cells so that you always have a fresh supply of skin.

The top part of your epidermis, the part you can see, is made of dried-up, dead epidermis cells. Those dried-up cells are always coming off . . . when you take a bath, when you put on clothes, and when you get a scratch. You'll never miss them because the special cells further inside keep making new skin.

Most of the time, the blood vessels near your scratch expand. When blood vessels expand, more blood can get to the scene of the injury. The extra blood makes your scratch look reddish.

The extra blood also brings thousands of extra white blood cells. And white blood cells are your body's army. In case any germs get through your skin, your white-blood-cell army is there to destroy them.

If there are no germs to fight, the white-blood-cell army goes away. The blood vessels go back to their normal size, and the redness disappears.

If your cut bleeds, you have cut through your epidermis into the next layer of skin—your dermis. Your dermis

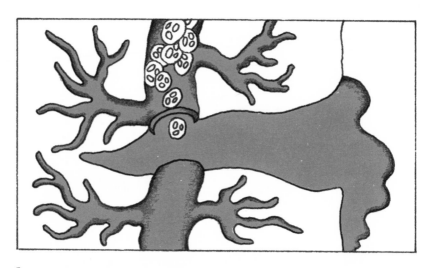

has so many tiny blood vessels that almost every time a cut gets into the dermis, you tear some of them. When a blood vessel is torn, blood comes out.

The blood that comes out may wash away the germs that got into your cut. But just in case some germs are still there, thousands of white blood cells rush to the scene, the way they do when you get a scratch. Their job: to destroy any invading germs.

At the same time that the white blood cells are fighting the germs, your body has to stop the bleeding. You have spe-

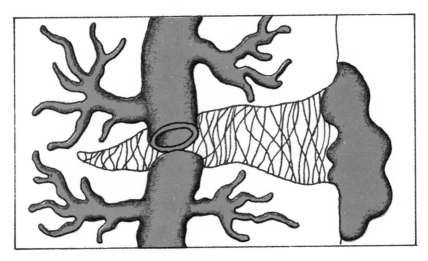

cial parts for that job. They're called platelets ... little plates ... because that's what they look like.

The little plates are very tiny and very delicate. They move around inside the blood vessels until they are needed. They know they're needed when they bump into the rough edges of a cut.

Blast! The platelets burst into lots of tiny pieces that stick to the edges of your cut. When the platelets break apart, it's a signal for the blood to make long, sticky threads. The threads weave a web in and around the platelets and across the cut.

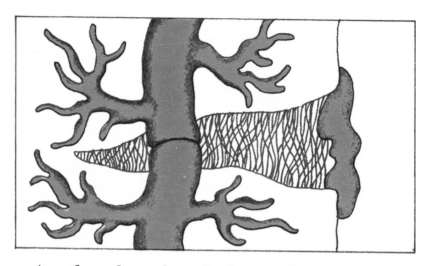

As the threads of the web get thicker and closer together, parts of your blood get caught in the web. Soon, the web is so thick that the blood can't get through at all, and the cut is all plugged up.

The outside of the plug, the part that touches the air, gets dried out and forms the scab.

Once the cut has a scab, all the broken parts underneath can start working to heal themselves. The germs that got inside are gobbled up and destroyed by the white blood cells. The broken blood vessels rebuild themselves. The injured dermis rebuilds itself. The epidermis cells that are always making more of themselves patch up your skin with new epidermis.

When the healing is finished, the scab falls off, and you can see the new skin underneath.

Most of the time, cuts take about a week to heal.

eye, something in it

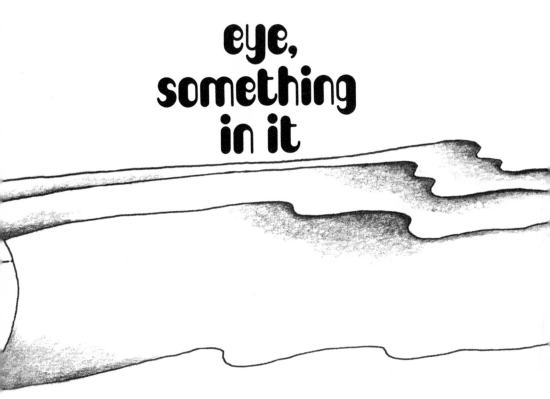

Usually, when anything comes near your eye, your eye closes. If a ball is zinging toward your face, your eye will close. If someone is about to punch you in the nose, your eye will close. You don't even have to think. Your eye just closes by itself. That's how your eye protects itself from injuries.

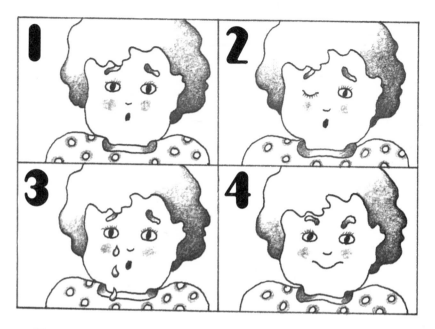

But sometimes the wind blows a speck of dust or sand that is so small your eye doesn't see it coming. Suddenly your eye feels funny. You can feel something in there, and it feels uncomfortable.

Your eye wants to get that speck out. First, your eyelid tries to push the speck out. Your eyelid closes and opens and closes and opens. When the lid slides over your eye, sometimes it pushes the speck down to the lower lid and out.

If the tiny speck won't be pushed, your eye will begin to make tears. Tears are the way your eye washes itself. When you have something in your eye, it's *good* to cry because crying makes even more tears. A flood of tears is like a lot of water washing your eye. Usually, the speck will float away.

Remember: don't rub your eye while there is something in it. If you do, the speck may scratch your eye.

You may notice tiny red lines in your eye. They are expanded blood vessels. The blood vessels expand so that your white-blood-cell army can rush to the scene just in case it has to fight the speck.

When the speck is washed out, the army is no longer needed. The extra blood—and the redness—go away.

goosebumps

Have you ever come out of a warm tub into cold air? Did you get little bumps all over your body? A lot of people call them *goosebumps*.

If you look very carefully at a goosebump, you'll find a hair coming out the middle of it. Your body is covered with little hairs. The root of each hair sits in a follicle, a tiny pocket in your skin.

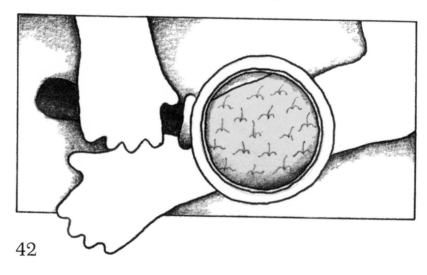

Most of the time, the hairs lie flat on your skin. But when you are cold, a tiny muscle pulls at the follicle that the hair is sitting in. That makes the hair stand up. It also makes the skin bunch into a little bump.

It seems like a silly thing to do ... especially since goosebumps don't make us any warmer. But scientists think that many years ago, goosebumps did make people warmer.

People were covered with lots more hair in those days. The hair on a person's body was longer and thicker than ours. When a person was cold, the little muscles made all those hairs stand up. When the hairs were up straight, the warm air from the person's body got trapped in the hairs. The person was protected from the cold by a blanket of warm air. Cats keep warm this way.

Today, people don't have such thick hair. And when *your* hair stands up, you don't get any warmer. But the muscle is still there, pulling those hairs up and causing goosebumps.

Goosebumps go away as soon as your body warms up.

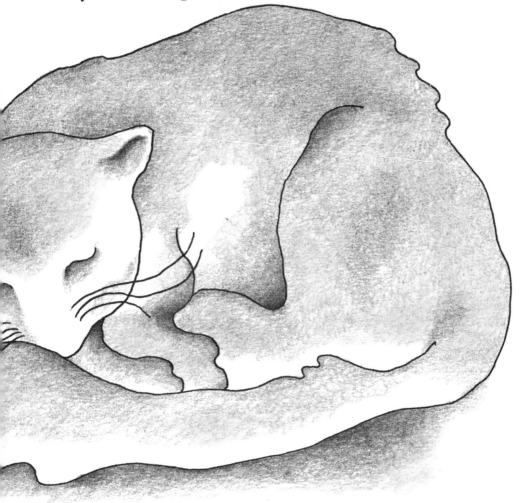

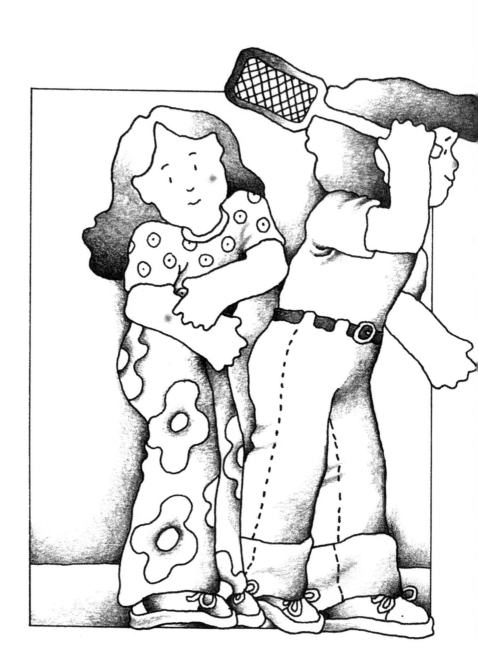

mosquito bite

Only female mosquitoes "bite." Actually they don't really bite; they can't even open their jaws! Instead, they stick their "stylets" into your skin and sip some blood.

Stylets are like tiny needles that the mosquito hides in her lower lip. When the stylets go in, some mosquito saliva goes in, too.

Mosquito saliva does a funny thing to your body. It makes histamines move around. Histamines are liquids that usually sit quietly inside tiny parts of your body called cells. If nothing bothers the histamines, they just sit there.

Mosquito saliva makes the histamines come out of the cells. They ooze around in the saliva, and they tickle some of your nerve endings. When nerve endings get tickled by histamines, they send an itch message. And that's why a mosquito bite itches.

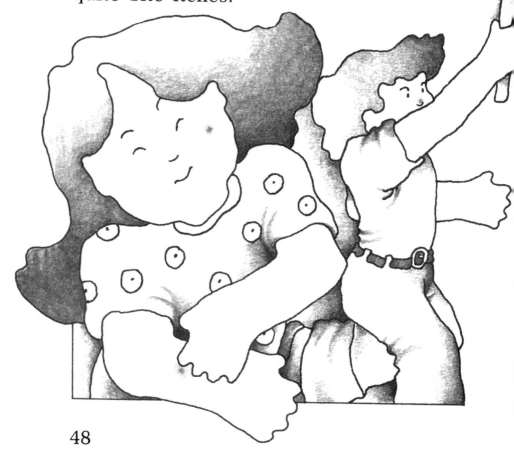

A mosquito bite also makes a lump. That's because as soon as the saliva got into your body, thousands of white blood cells rushed to the spot.

A lot of white blood cells are needed to get rid of that mosquito saliva. Thousands of them squirm out of your blood vessels in clear, yellow plasma. When the histamines are oozing around, they cause even more plasma and white blood cells to come out. The white blood cells gobble up the mosquito saliva and make it disappear.

The lump on your skin that you call a mosquito bite is caused by the extra plasma and white blood cells all crowded together—just as in a bee sting.

When the saliva has been gobbled up, the white blood cells and the plasma go away and the mosquito bite disappears.

nosebleed

The skin on the inside of your nose is very, very thin. Besides thin skin, your nose also has extra blood vessels.

Noses bleed easily. They can bleed from blowing too hard or from a big sneeze or from a poke. Just a tiny scratch inside your nose can tear blood vessels. When blood vessels in your nose are torn, you get a nosebleed.

A nosebleed heals the same way a cut heals. The cut will get plugged up, and a scab will form on top.

One problem with a nosebleed is that the scab comes off easily. The inside of your nose is so moist that the scab doesn't get very hard. Sometimes it comes off when you blow your nose or bump it or poke it. Then you get the same nosebleed from the same blood vessel . . . all over again.

Once your nosebleed stops, be careful!

pins and needles

Sometimes, when you sit for a long time in a funny position, you get a prickly feeling in your foot or in your hand. You feel as though millions of tiny pins and needles are running on your skin.

The "pins and needles" are a warning. A fire engine uses its siren to warn cars to get out of the way. "Pins and needles" are like a siren warning you that it's time to change your position.

Some very important parts of your body are getting squashed.

Blood vessels are getting squashed. Your blood moves inside blood vessels delivering food to all parts of your body. If some of those blood vessels are getting squashed, then some parts of your body are not getting food.

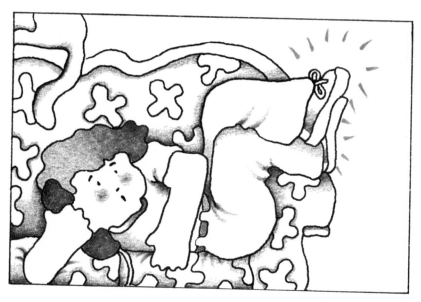

Nerves are getting squashed too. Nerves are long, skinny messengers that deliver messages to and from your brain. Your funny position is pressing on some of those nerves.

Scientists think that it is a combination of the squashed blood vessels and the squashed nerves that causes "pins and needles." The cure is easy. All you have to do is straighten out your body. When everything gets going again, the "pins and needles" will go away.

splinter

Splinters are usually tiny bits of wood that break through your skin and stay there.

A piece of wood doesn't belong in your skin, so your body sends its army of white blood cells to fight the splinter.

56

White blood cells are good fighters.
They try to destroy any strange thing
that gets into your body. But a splinter
is too big. There is no way that white
blood cells can get rid of a splinter. If it
is left in, your body keeps sending more
and more white blood cells. So many of
them crowd into that one little spot that
it gets reddish and hot. The lump of
white blood cells pushes hard on your
nerve endings. Ouch, your body needs
help! Somebody has to pull the splinter
out.

When the splinter is out, the white
blood cells gobble up any leftover germs
that may have sneaked into your body
with the splinter.

stitches and scars

Sometimes, because a cut is very deep, the two sides of the cut are separated a lot. Your body has to make a huge amount of new skin to fill up the hole. And you probably will get a scar. In order to understand what causes scars, you will have to know about cells.

Your body is made of trillions of tiny things called "cells"—cells that are skinny, cells that are fat. Sticky cells, rubbery cells, red cells, white cells.

Each part of you has its own special cells. The top part of your skin is made of epidermis cells. The inside of your skin, your dermis, is made of several kinds of cells.

Like many other cells in your body, epidermis and dermis cells are always making more of themselves. When you get a small cut, your epidermis and dermis cells do a good job of replacing your injured parts. After the cut has healed, you can't even tell where it was.

But sometimes you get a cut that makes a big hole in your skin. Filling that hole is a huge job. Special cells called fibroblasts take over.

Fibroblasts are fast workers. They work so fast that they fill up the hole without leaving much room at all for the other epidermis and dermis cells.

Fibroblasts are a different shape and a different color and a different size from the rest of your skin cells. When fibroblasts make most of the cells that fill up a hole, you have a scar.

If the two sides of the hole are brought closer together, your body won't have to work so hard to fill up the hole with new skin. And if you get a scar, it will be a tiny one.

Sometimes the doctor uses a special tape to bring the sides of the cut together. Other times, the doctor stitches the sides together with a special thread.

A cut that is taped or stitched heals the same way as any other cut.

After a week or two, your cut skin will stay together by itself. Then the doctor can remove the tape or take out the stitches.

don't
stop here

Now that you've learned a little bit about how your body works, you probably have more questions than you had before.
Keep asking.
Ask your parents.
Ask your doctor.
Ask anybody who will help you find answers.

If you ask a lot of questions and read a lot of books, you'll discover something very important: There are many unanswered questions.

A lot more research has to be done. Perhaps you will become one of the scientists whose questions and research will help us understand more about the human body.

frequently used words and their meanings

EPIDERMIS—the outside part of the skin.

DERMIS—the inside part of the skin. There are many blood vessels and nerve endings in the dermis.

NERVE ENDINGS—tiny stringy things that send messages to your brain.

BLOOD VESSELS—tiny hoses in the body that carry blood.

PLASMA—the clear yellow, watery part of the blood.

WHITE BLOOD CELLS—parts of the blood. Along with red blood cells, they travel in blood vessels. They have two very important jobs. They are the body's army and its garbage collectors.